AWAKEN
The Search is Over

Natalie Grueninger
& Karina Machado

Copyright © 2016 by Natalie Grueninger & Karina Machado

All rights reserved.

No part of this book may be reproduced in any form or by any electronic or mechanical means including information storage and retrieval systems, without permission in writing from the authors. The only exception is by a reviewer, who may quote short excerpts in a review.

All quotes from A Course in Miracles © are from the Third Edition, published in 2007. They are used with permission from the copyright holder and publisher, the Foundation for Inner Peace, P.O. Box 598, Mill Valley, CA 94942-0598, www.acim.org and info@acim.org.

ISBN 978-0-646-95942-9

Cover and book design by Kathryn Holeman / kshcreative.com

For all our teachers, living and in the spirit world, thank you, thank you, thank you.

Genesis 2:21

And the Lord God caused a deep sleep to fall upon Adam, and he slept...

Our time has come.
Awaken!

INTRODUCTION

*We are spirit sisters, you and I.
You may think that we are strangers
but in fact, we are family.*

Some of us weren't blessed with a sister, so we have to find our own.
—KYLIE MCGIRR

Dear Spirit Sister,

On a day trip to the Blue Mountains, in NSW, one blue-sky autumn day in 2015, we toured the Jenolan Caves, one of the most breathtaking cave formations in the world. Inside a section known as the Cathedral Cave, the guide explained how early explorers had filed into the ancient space by candlelight. As their

AWAKEN

small, fickle flames illumined only the tiny area around them, the explorers initially thought they'd discovered a humble cavern, never imagining they were specks in a vast underground labyrinth that stretched wide across the earth, like the giant roots of a gnarled old tree.

Like those myopic explorers, we too are in danger of seeing only what's revealed to us in the small pool of light we cast about ourselves as we go about our everyday lives, as if asleep. But, just as those adventurers, by extending their light, eventually came to appreciate the marvel that contained them, we too can awaken to the breadth of life that's ours to explore. Like those men in the caves, we must learn to look beyond our meagre puddles of light and shine our lanterns of consciousness in every direction so that we know what we stand in. Only then will we see what has always been there, blocked by the shadows of our limiting beliefs.

INTRODUCTION

These shadows—fears—stand between us and our remembrance of our own magnificence and power: our connection to God or Source. It doesn't matter what you call this higher power that's inside each of us—call it your Higher-Self, Spirit, the Universe, the Infinite, All That Is, or whatever you prefer. What's important is that you remember your connection to it, and understand that when you're "unplugged" from it, as we call it, life cannot flow smoothly.

However, when you're "plugged in" to remembering the sacred part of you, blessings follow as naturally as flowers open to the sun.

To help stay "plugged in," it's essential to have a daily spiritual practice. Ours is a morning ritual we adore, and share here for you to perhaps use as a springboard to discover your own way. Waking early to the day, we say 'thank you.' After meditating for 20 minutes to Wayne Dyer's I Am meditation, we pray—one of our favourites is St. Francis of Assisi's "Make me an instrument of your peace . . ." —and read other inspirational texts (for example, *A Course in Miracles* and Mark Nepo's *The Book of Awakening*), before going for a walk. Breathing in the morning air, tipping our faces to the sky, connecting to the trees, birds and water, is like charging our batteries for the day ahead. Yes, you need to wake early for this, but we've found it to be beyond worth it, rather, utterly transformational.

Awakened to our inner lives, our hearts burst with gratitude every day—rain or shine, through tears of joy or hardship—because we've learned to search within, and what we've found there is treasure. You too have treasure inside you and we've written this book to help you find your way to it. You'll discover that for as long as you've drawn breath, your soul has been leaving clues—like crumbs scattered to help you find your way home—that will put you

INTRODUCTION

on *your* path to freedom, wholeness and happiness.

The pages that follow will gently nudge you to wake up from your slumber, to remember the sacred centre you may have forgotten, though it is the most powerful part of you. Opening your eyes to the light that's always been within, you'll awaken to a bright, new dawn made beautiful by your own wondrous potential.

This book serves three purposes: to celebrate the infinite possibilities to bring joy, peace and contentment to our lives that, until now, have been dancing in the dark of our sleeping minds; to help light your way to your new, awakened, life; and to remind you that you are not alone, ever! We are sisters but that bond can be found beyond blood ties. Know this: There's an entire sisterhood of women sharing that space in your heart where your deepest self dwells, sharing your loves, hopes, fears and dreams.

Consider *Awaken* your portable tribe. Keep it in your bag and open it at random when you need a fix of soul nourishment, or read it from start to finish. And then use the hashtags #Awaken, #portabletribe, and #Soulnourishment to tell us about how it's helping you find your way back to remembering who you are.

Now, get ready to rub the sleep from your eyes. Yawn, stretch and shift your perception, turn your focus inward and take the first step back on the path to your soul. We're holding the lantern for you.

Love,
Karina and Natalie

The breeze at dawn has secrets to tell you.
Don't go back to sleep.
You must ask for what you really want.
Don't go back to sleep.

—Rumi

What is it that
you really want?

What makes the butterflies
dance in your belly?

What lights the lamps
in your heart?

You must begin
where you are,
and here you are.

Why do you weep?

Because I remember...

What do you remember?

Home.

It too remembers you.

You are enough.

Do you hear me?

You are.

Close your eyes,
breathe in
and see infinity.

Deep inside you is a vast and infinite source of peace and bliss that you can access at anytime, by simply closing your eyes and being still.

Cast off your human cloak and don't be afraid to show yourself.

You are loved.

You are love.

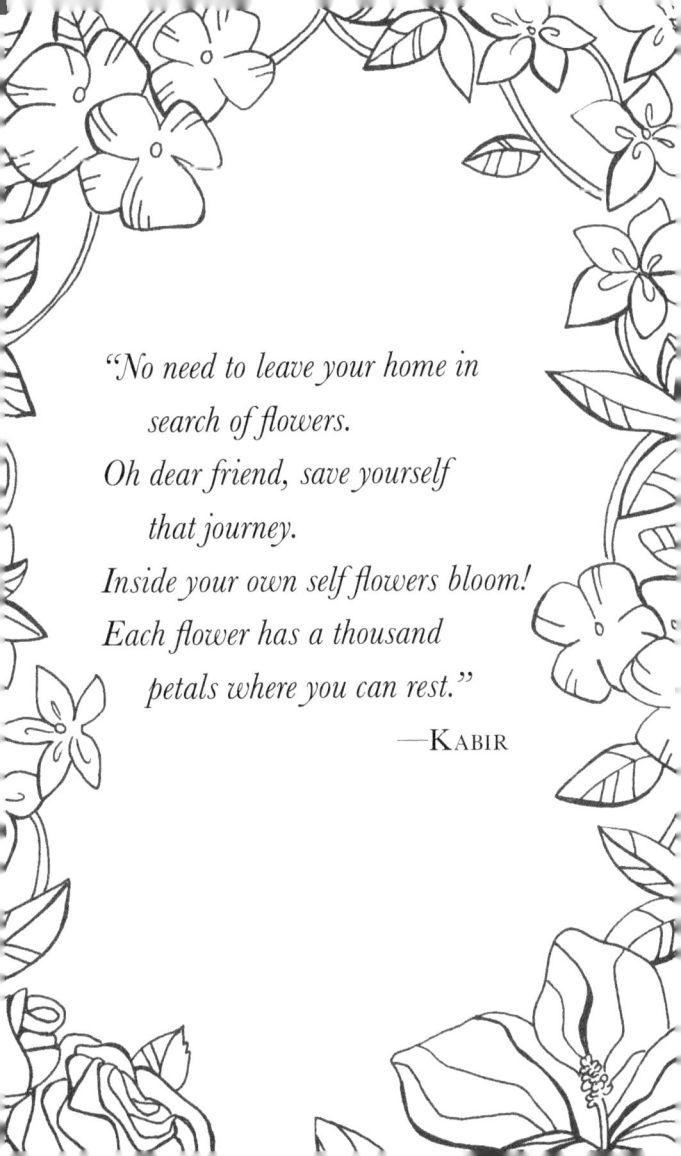

*"No need to leave your home in search of flowers.
Oh dear friend, save yourself that journey.
Inside your own self flowers bloom!
Each flower has a thousand petals where you can rest."*

—Kabir

Sleeping we wonder
is this all there is?

Awake we see there is
much, much more.

Don't despair.

Trust.

All is well.

You are not alone.

We are with you.

You are beautiful.

You have something important to give.

The world needs you.

Yes, you.

That dream you have?

We know it matters.

And yes, you can!

Spirit Sister, do not delay.

You know what it is you need to do.

Begin.

Are you haunted by a sense that there's something you've forgotten?

Look within.

It's you.

You've been there all along.

"*Who looks outside dreams;*
who looks inside wakes."

—C.G. Jung

Listen.

You are limitless.

Break free!

That feeling — that you can't go on this way?

Don't ignore it.

It's a call from home.

Is any of what we see real?

No.

Love is all that's real.

Love.

Focus only on the good, on the light, on the love, and watch miracles unfold.

Spirit Sister, that which you love, do more of it.

There is no separation.

We are in you
and you are in us.

We don't have all the
answers and that's okay.

Listen to your inner guide,
it knows the way.

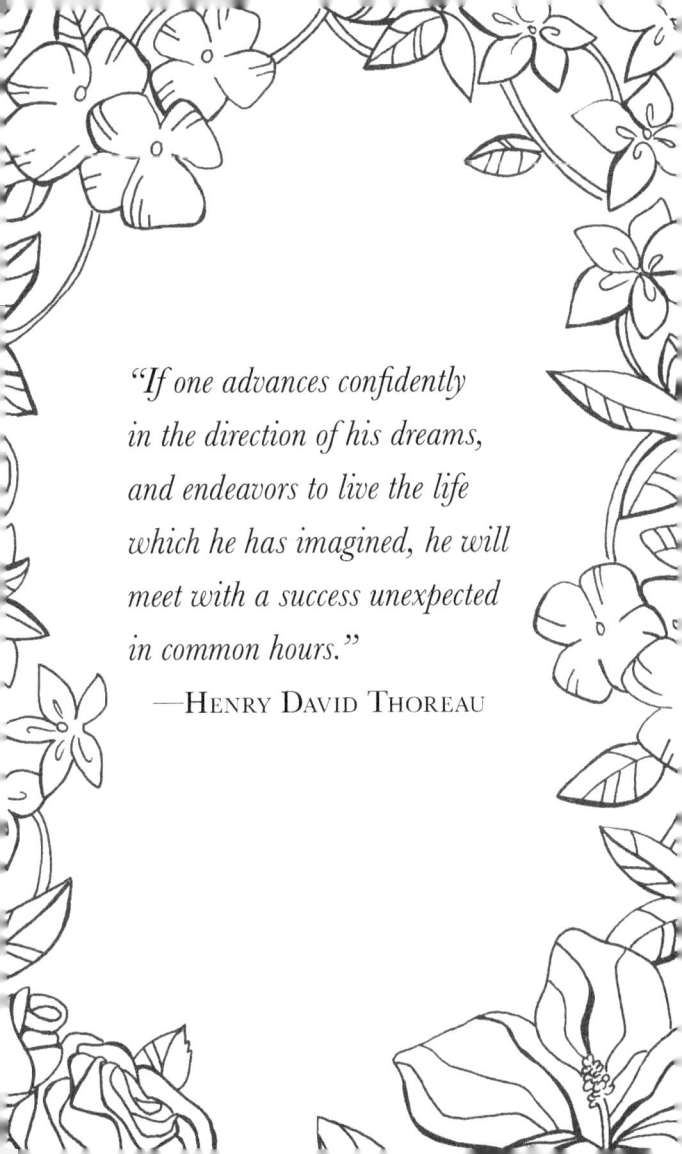

"If one advances confidently in the direction of his dreams, and endeavors to live the life which he has imagined, he will meet with a success unexpected in common hours."

—Henry David Thoreau

Your feelings are signposts.

When you feel good you are on the path, when you don't you have detoured.

No more excuses.

No more explanations.

Answer the call.

The world flows from you.

Everything is connected.

Look around you.

The world needs your light.

We know it's hard
at times but we're all
behind you.

If only you could see yourself how we see you.

Magnificent and poised to soar!

Like a rose in full bloom,
Surrender to the full sun
of your soul.

Banish doubt, Sister.

Anchor yourself in love
and there is
nothing to fear.

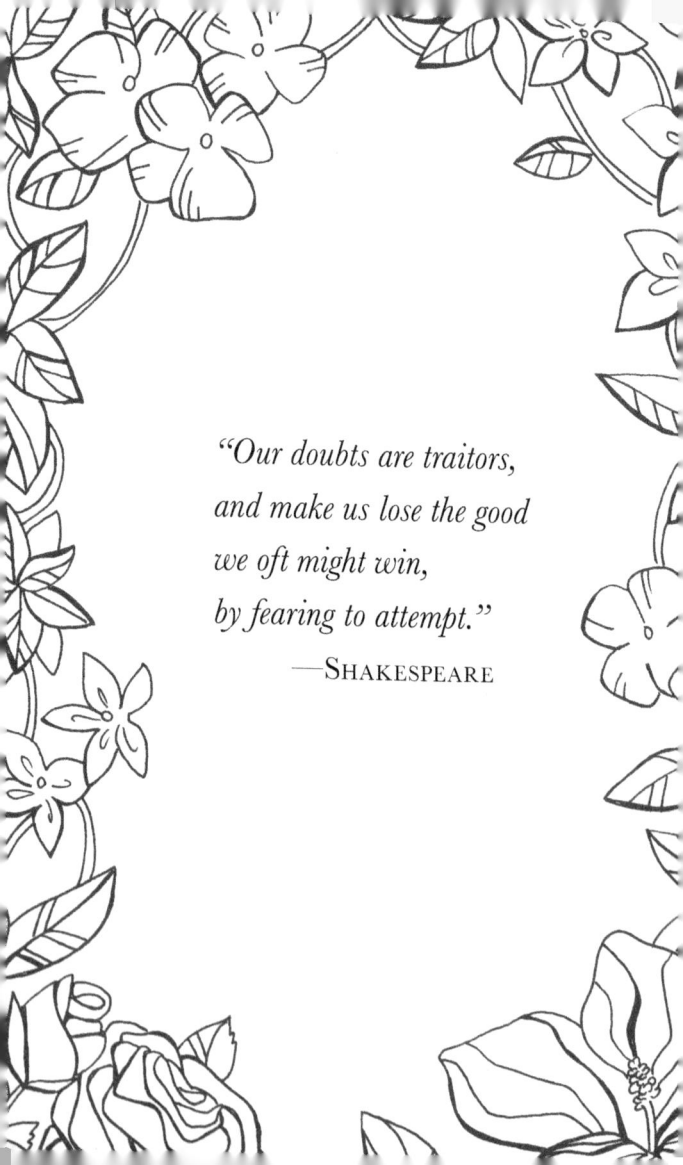

"*Our doubts are traitors,
and make us lose the good
we oft might win,
by fearing to attempt.*"

—SHAKESPEARE

We go about our days as
if we are here for infinity,
when really—
on this earthly plane—
we have but a short time.

There was a lesson in what you went through.

Hold your experience up like a jewel and see how the light shines through.

You are in charge of your peace.

Always choose love.

There is so much to be grateful for today.

Spirit Sister, we all stumble, there is no shame in that.

Take my hand and rise.

You're starting
to see it now,
aren't you?

Your wings are your imagination.

Leave sleep behind and fly into a bright new world.

Cut the ties that bind you to your old perceptions.

Wake up and know you already are who you want to be.

Greet her with a smile.

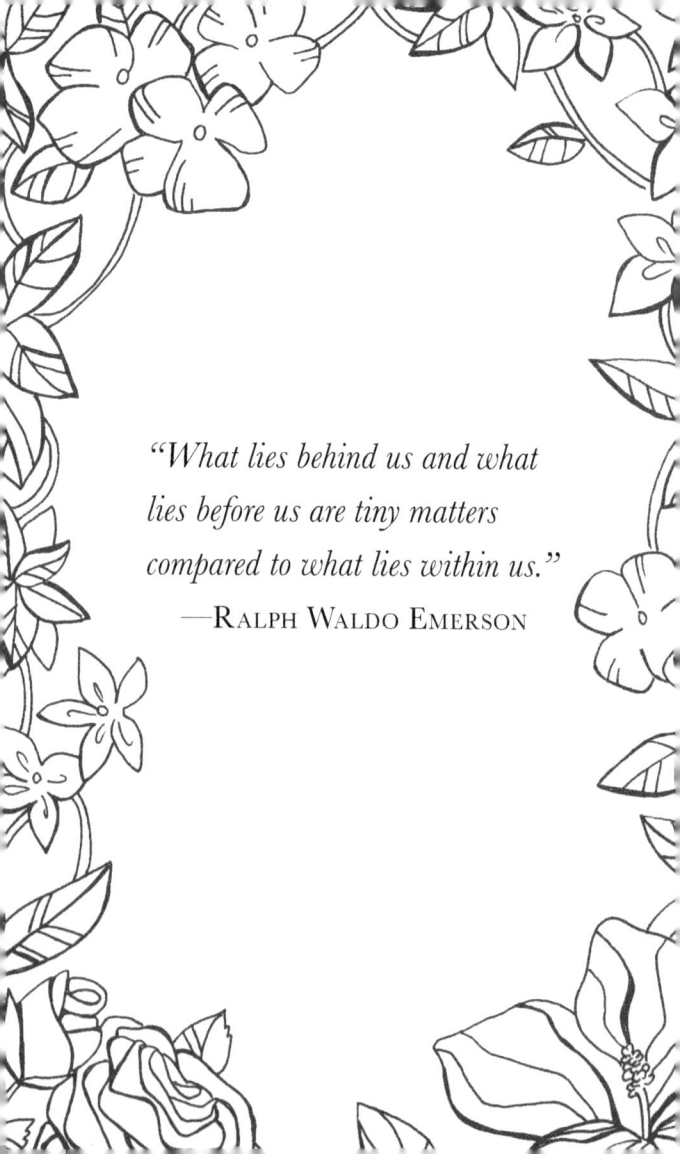

"What lies behind us and what lies before us are tiny matters compared to what lies within us."

—Ralph Waldo Emerson

Make no mistake, Sister.

Joy is a choice.

What's burning inside you?

Follow the light of the flame.

Be aware of your thoughts.

Focus on those that expand feelings of peace, love and oneness.

You are a
powerful creator.

Do you realise this?

All in good time.

Accept that there are mysteries that will never be solved.

That is part of the richness of our human experience.

Awaken and know that love never dies.

Don't put it off any longer.

Forgive.

"Listen,—perhaps you catch a hint of an ancient state not quite forgotten; dim, perhaps, and yet not altogether unfamiliar, like a song whose name is long forgotten, and the circumstances in which you heard completely unremembered. Not the whole song has stayed with you, but just a little wisp of melody, attached not to a person or a place or anything in particular. But you remember, from just this little part, how lovely was the song, how wonderful the setting where you heard it, and how you loved those who were there and listened with you."

—A COURSE IN MIRACLES
(ACIM T-21.I.6.)

Honour your soul.

Spend quiet time with yourself everyday.

Make time today
to be in nature.

Marvel at the sunrise,
a bird in flight or the
rolling waves.

Ask yourself,
how can I serve?

You are a spark
of the divine here
on earth.

You make a difference.

Take the path of least resistance.

Surrender.

Be like a lighthouse shining bright in all weather, guiding others home.

"Let yourself be silently drawn by the strange pull of what you really love. It will not lead you astray."

—Rumi

Believe in yourself.

Nothing is beyond your reach.

Yes, this is the sign you've been waiting for.

Treat yourself like you would a beloved friend.

Be kind, be gentle, be loving.

There are no limits to
what you can create.

Spirit Sister, shed the human armour.

Reveal the beauty and wisdom that is within.

The wisdom of the ages is always available to you.

All you need do is say:

Guide me.

And then, listen.

Just make a start.

Accept that in our human guise we are vulnerable.

It's okay to ask for help.

"*All shall be well, and all shall be well and all manner of thing shall be well.*"

—Julian of Norwich

Trust in your intuition.

Spirit Sister,
miracles await you.

When you wake up in the morning, let thank you be the first words you utter.

There is no time to waste.

Make the change you've been dreaming of.

Know that things can improve.

Treasure today.

You deserve to live the life you've dreamed of.

You're worthy of it!

You are not limited by another person's success.

There is enough to go around.

See the abundance.

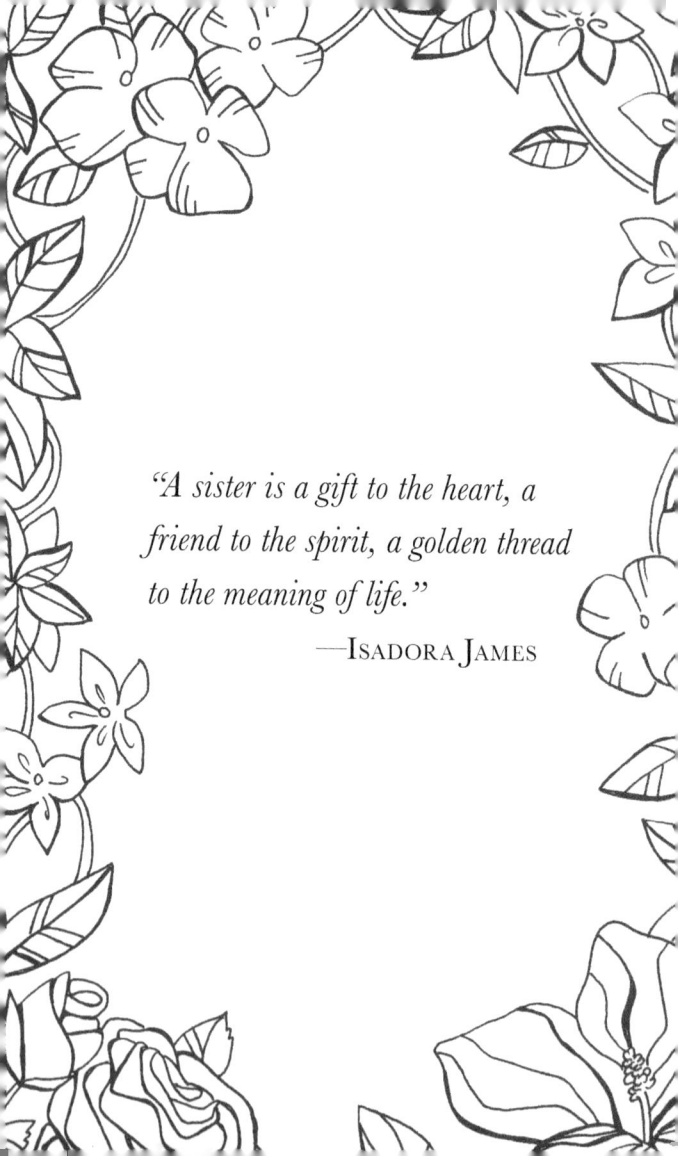

"A sister is a gift to the heart, a friend to the spirit, a golden thread to the meaning of life."

—Isadora James

Listen carefully to the stories you tell yourself and others, for they create your reality.

Making your wellbeing a priority is not an act of selfishness, it is essential for living the life you want.

Release what no longer serves you.

All this, yes, all of it,
is part of the plan.

You have the power to bring your ideas to life.

You've heard it said before, Sister, you are not your past, you are not defined by your perceived mistakes.

Each dawn brings with it a fresh start and another opportunity to acknowledge the real You.

You are a spiritual
being having a human
experience.

Say this out loud,
over and over, until
it solidifies.

Share your knowledge freely, support your fellow man, celebrate the success of others.

There is no lack.

*"What if you slept
And what if
In your sleep
You dreamed
And what if
In your dream
You went to heaven
And there plucked a strange
    and beautiful flower
And what if
When you awoke
You had that flower in
    your hand
Ah, what then?"*

—Samuel Taylor Coleridge

You have the power
to transform your life
simply by changing your
thoughts, the intentions
you make, and the way
you look at things.

Spirit Sister, the universe likes to play a game of vibration snap, where it responds to the vibrations you emit by sending you a perfect match.

Send out only high, empowering, loving vibes, and watch as the universe showers you with miracles.

Base all your decisions in love.

This is the key.

We know that
sometimes you feel the
more you walk down
this mystical path, the
more questions you have.

That's okay.

It's a sign that
you're waking from
your long sleep.

The universe is supported by a superior power—call it God, Source, Light, or Spirit, the label is not what's important.

This all-encompassing love, loves you unconditionally.

The same infinite wisdom and love that created the universe wants you, needs you, to fulfill your purpose.

It will look out for you if you open your heart, let go and trust.

Watch for the signs, Sister.

Signs that the universe loves and supports you.

They are there.

Those mind-blowing questions you've been pondering: Why am I here? What is my purpose in life? Where was I before I came here?

We think about them too.

Turn them over to God, and listen with your heart for the answer.

"*Let the beauty we love be what we do. There are hundreds of ways to kneel and kiss the ground.*"

—Rumi

The only courage you need, is the courage to be You.

In every moment, in every instant, do what feels right, do what feels light.

We are teetering on the
brink of greatness,
do you feel it?

We know how much you desire it. Don't concern yourself with the 'how's'. Do something today, however small, to align yourself with it.

Go now!

Throw off your weary disguises!

We see who you really are.

Be you!

Surrender, trust and detach from the outcome.

This is the only way.

There is nothing else you need to become complete.

You are perfect.

You are whole.

Know that.

Rub the sleep from your eyes and see the miracles that surround you.

Do not allow the vision to become blurred.

There's no need for you to keep explaining yourself.

"When you are inspired by some great purpose, some extraordinary project, all your thoughts break their bonds: Your mind transcends limitations, your consciousness expands in every direction, and you find yourself in a new, great and wonderful world. Dormant forces, faculties and talents become alive, and you discover yourself to be a greater person by far than you ever dreamed yourself to be."

—Patanjali

There is nothing missing.

Give up comparisons!

You are no better or worse than any other person.

We are all divine.

Release all negativity.

Another person's success does not impede yours.

What you share with
the world returns to you
in spades.

Gracefully accept what is.

Spirit Sister, stop trying
to force things into being.

The harder you try,
the more you push
them away.

What you chase after will continue to run from you.

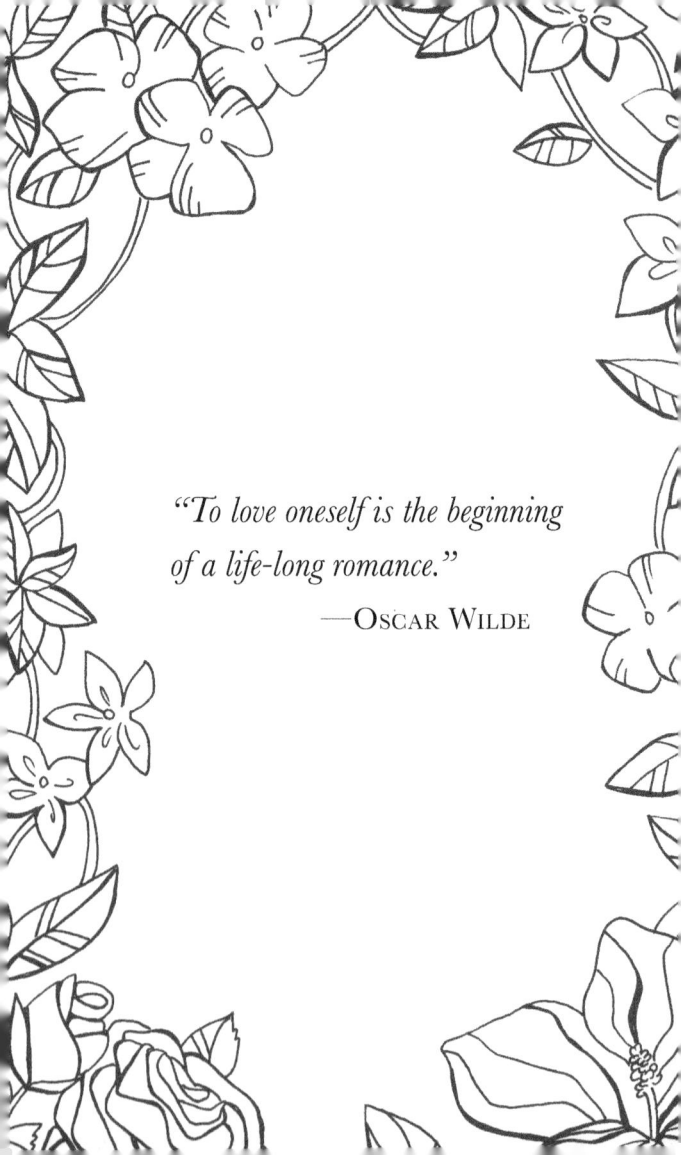

"To love oneself is the beginning of a life-long romance."

—Oscar Wilde

When you are on purpose, you act from a place of love and your focus is on serving and giving, not on what's in it for you.

Once you begin walking
the spiritual path,
the right people and
circumstances will begin
to appear. Have faith.

Trust the inner guidance you receive and banish the urge to explain it or justify it to others.

Refrain from thinking and saying things that you don't want to manifest in your physical reality.

Be for things that you'd like to see more of in the world, rather than against things you'd like to experience less of.

Be for love.
Be for peace.
Be for health.

There's not a second to waste in anything unloving.

Not a second!

Music and smells bypass the ego and speak directly to the soul.

They help lead us home.

Do not underestimate the power of your imagination.

It gives form to your dreams.

It is vital that you carve out time each day to reconnect with nature.

You who seek God, apart, apart
The thing you seek, thou art,
thou art.

—RUMI

Commit today to a daily spiritual practice.

This is crucial.

Many awaken only when brought to their knees in despair, or grief.

What if you could wake up before that day?

We know you can.

We have.

Take a step towards fulfilling the longings of your soul.

To delay is to wither.

The behaviour of others often mirrors our hidden depths.

Before condemning, reach inside to find what toxic crumbs you may be harbouring that echo what's distressing you.

Draw out those crumbs and scatter them on the wind.

Shed your former skins.
Be reborn every day.

Your experiences create the whole of your Self. Even the rotten ones— they are like compost nourishing the soil of your life.

Without the contrast of experiences, there is no way to learn and grow.

Nestled deep within, you carry the embryo of your own potential.

You are on a precipice.

Yet you will not fall,
but fly.

A treasure inside you
is waiting to crack the
hard ground of your fears
and shoot up, up, up to
the light.

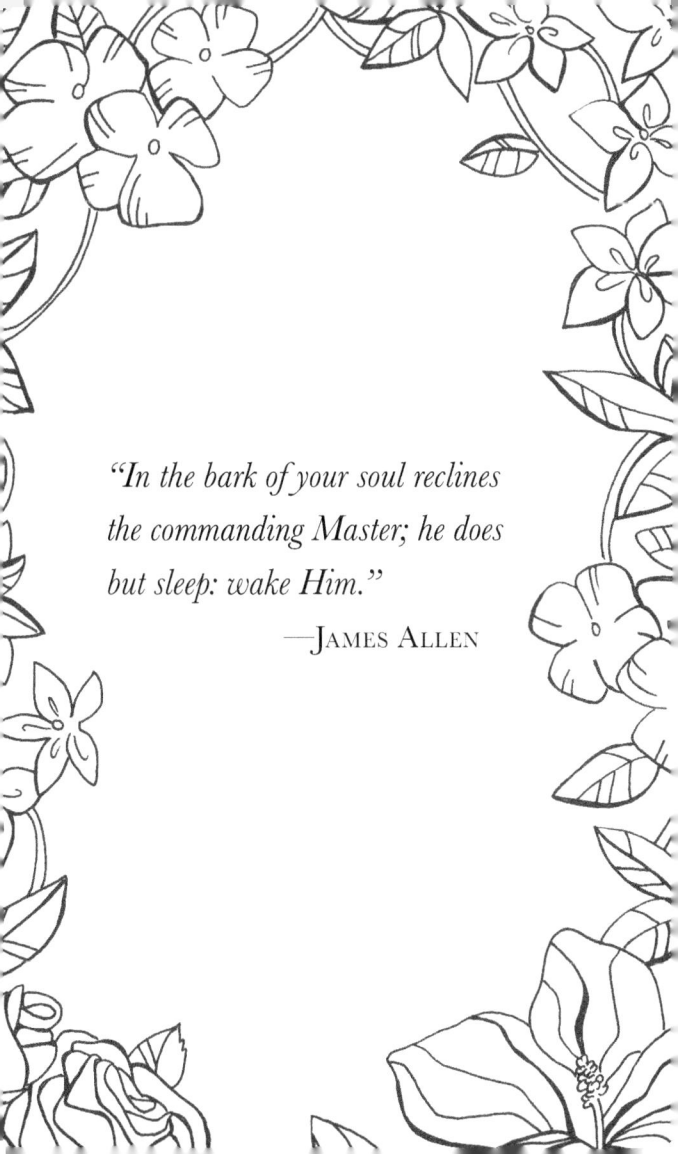

"*In the bark of your soul reclines the commanding Master; he does but sleep: wake Him.*"

—James Allen

Do you feel poised between two worlds?

This means you're close, oh so close, to stepping into your authentic self.

What do you have an affinity for?

Take heed.

That resonance links past, present and future.

It points the way to soul growth.

To awaken is to begin to remember.

In forgiveness there is absolute freedom.

Rest in humility.

Everything is aglow with indescribable beauty, if only you would see it.

Be prepared to find gifts
in places you don't expect.

When you begin to awaken, Spirit will push you to act on pursuing what you love. The more you delay, the more disconnected from Spirit—thus yourself— you become.

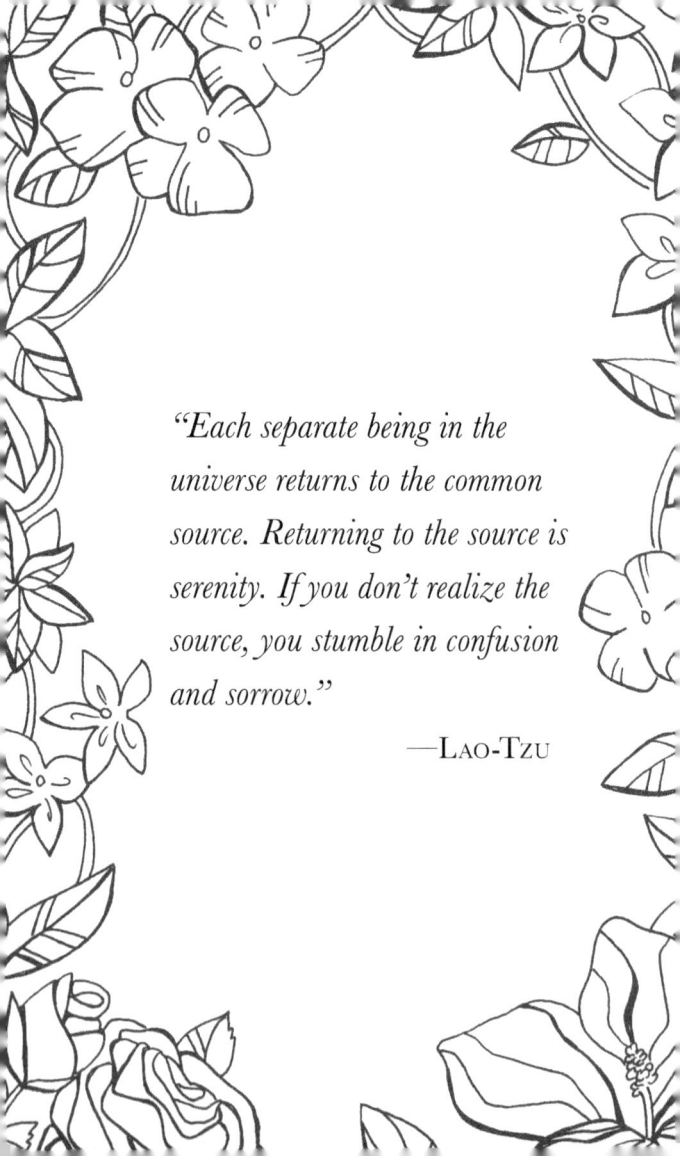

"Each separate being in the universe returns to the common source. Returning to the source is serenity. If you don't realize the source, you stumble in confusion and sorrow."

—Lao-Tzu

Spirit sister, you are a piece of God here on Earth.

When a storm blows through your life, be the lighthouse that stands solid and steady as the turbulent sea lashes against it—and know the sun will shine again.

Ask God for help and do not despair that your prayers have gone unanswered, for the miracle has been set in motion.

Be patient and allow the magic to unfold.

Spirit Sister, your sorrows and circumstances do not define you.

You are noble as the trees. Ever reaching skyward from their cradle of dirt, they pour blossoms like blessings onto the earth.

Your spiritual home is love in its purest form, the ultimate safe haven.

Take shelter there.

As hard as it is to accept at times, we are not responsible for any other person's happiness, not even that of our partners and children.

We can only live our own truth, shine our light brightly and help illuminate the way home.

Spirit Sister,
please forgive.

Not to let the other person off the hook but to free yourself.

The fact that you recognise that you acted from a place of fear means that you're awakening.

Rejoice in that!

We cannot change other people.

We can only point out the escape hatch and help light the way.

A spiritual life is the antidote to every fear.

"With life as fleeting as a halfdrawn breath, you have no need to plant anything but love."
—Rumi

A malnourished soul is difficult to hear.

Feed your soul music, poetry, love and landscapes.

Fill it with beauty and the call will grow louder.

Create fearlessly!

Do not concern yourself with how others will react to your work.

This has nothing to do with you.

Your need to be right is keeping you in the dark.

Eventually, we will all arrive at the same destination, although only some of us purposefully, with eyes wide open.

The path we take to get there is uniquely ours.

Make it count.

Leave room for the universe to surprise you.

Do not succumb to helplessness!

Together, we can heal our world.

Laugh heartily,
laugh unabashedly,
laugh often.

While on earth, your body is your soul's home and guardian.

Take good care of this miraculous and sacred vehicle.

Fall in love with it, for without it, your divinity would be unable to express itself in this world.

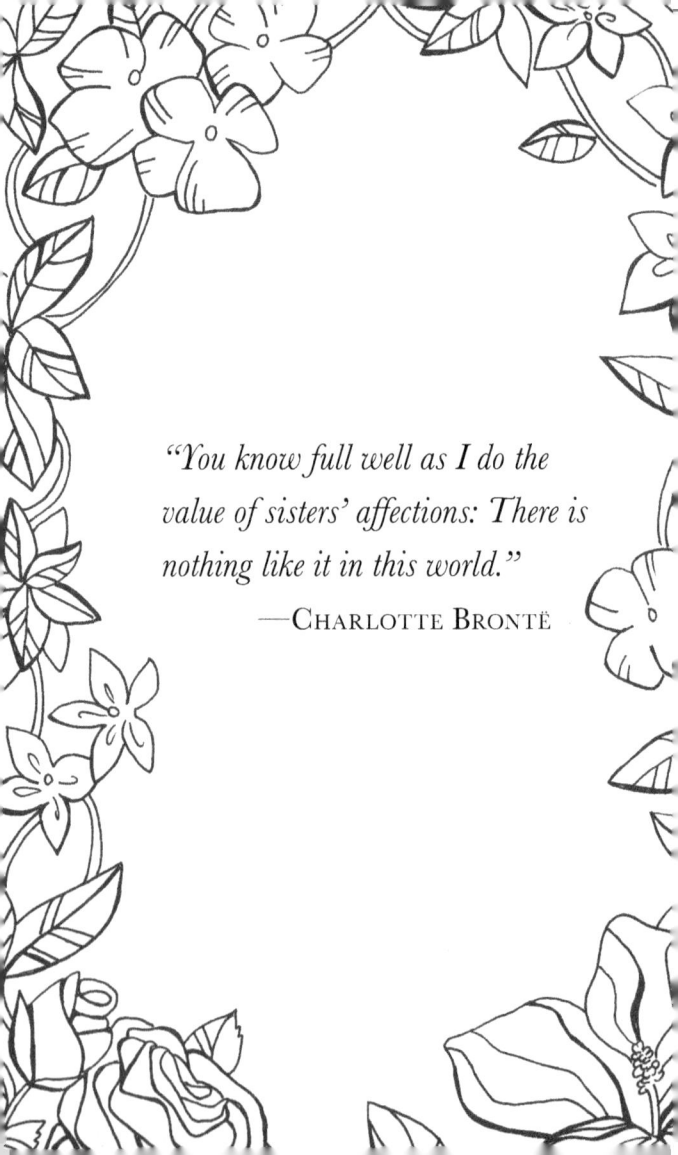

"You know full well as I do the value of sisters' affections: There is nothing like it in this world."

—Charlotte Brontë

You need not seek any other person's approval.

All you need is within you.

Trust.

Your senses can help lead you home.

They are gateways to the soul.

Attune yourself to their ancient guidance.

Spirit Sister, you are here for a reason, to share a unique gift with the world.

Cast fear aside and awaken to your destiny!

Beauty awakens the dormant soul and reveals a truth many have long forgotten — that the journey inwards is the only journey you need make.

That the internal, invisible world where your soul dwells, waits and longs for your return.

Spirit Sister, all our struggles arise from forgetting our connection to the Divine.

Remember you are magnificent, powerful and supported by an infinite invisible world.

Return often to the shelter of the silence within, it is a powerful teacher.

In love and humility, we share these truths with you through our pen, which carries the pulse of our beating hearts.

Now pick up your instrument, and share your truth.

One small step.

Afterword

We're honoured you've purchased our book. Our heartfelt wish is that it's served to help awaken you to a wondrous new life that's bursting with possibilities. As mentioned in the introduction, we'd love to hear from you. Our websites, email addresses and social media details are below. Use the hashtags #Awaken, #portabletribe, and #Soulnourishment to connect.

Love,
Karina and Natalie

www.facebook.com/Awakenthesearchisover

Karinamachado.com
www.facebook.com/Karina-Machado-226647390718696
TWITTER: @KMachadoAuthor
INSTAGRAM: karinamachadoauthor
EMAIL: karinamachado@optusnet.com.au

www.facebook.com/nataliegrueningerauthor
TWITTER: @OntheTudorTrail
INSTAGRAM: themosthappy78
EMAIL: ngrueninger@optusnet.com.au

www.ingramcontent.com/pod-product-compliance
Lightning Source LLC
Chambersburg PA
CBHW051945290426
44110CB00015B/2112